IDENTIFYING
BUTTONS

Alan and Gillian Meredith
Michael J. Cuddeford

Mount Publications

Produced and Published by Mount Publications

© Mount Publications 1997

ISBN 1 900571 02 1

Mount Publications,
PO Box 1916,
Chelmsford,
Essex.
CM3 1EY.
England.

CONTENTS

INTRODUCTION

Buttons have a long history, going back perhaps even as far as the Bronze Age. However, because their function generally dictates their form, their overall appearance has remained largely unchanged.

The study of buttons is ongoing, and archaeological research remains the best source for dating early types. Even with later buttons however, identification can provide something of a challenge. Few buttons are produced by any central authority, and the only records that may be kept of types and designs can be lost or destroyed when firms either close down, or are taken over by larger ones. As a result, it is quite possible to come across buttons only thirty or forty years old that bear initials or motifs that are now complete mysteries. This means that anyone with a desire to conduct original research will always have plenty of opportunity, from scouring the archives of the large button makers to consulting old regional trade directories in an attempt to date and attribute certain examples.

Although some buttons may be plain utilitarian objects, others can be miniature works of art reflecting fashions and styles of times gone by. Uniform buttons, both military and civilian, represent several centuries of national and social history. As a result, buttons are widely collected The most popular types of button sought by collectors are not unnaturally the more decorative sorts, with uniform buttons also being much in demand. Yet despite this popularity, there have been relatively few books published that look at the subject in a general sense. This book is certainly not a definitive corpus of buttons. Indeed, no single volume could ever serve that purpose, as many types of button would require an entire catalogue to themselves. What we have set out to do is to present a broad overview of most button categories and types, with representative examples showing particular characteristics and styles. Thus anyone needing to identify a particular example can narrow down the possibilities sufficiently to provide a general identification and date. Given the restrictions of a book this size, we have limited the inclusion of uniform buttons to British examples only, but we have included an appendix covering French military buttons in order to widen the scope a little more.

Acknowledgements: The authors are greatly indebted to Stan Godsell, who permitted us to photograph many items from his collection. We also gratefully acknowledge the contribution of Yann Ledru and David Smith, and the assistance of Jim Patterson, Paul Withers and the British Button Society. We would recommend membership of the British Button Society to anyone with an interest in the study or collection of buttons.

Illustrations: All photographs are reproduced at approximately actual size.

1.

HISTORICAL   BACKGROUND

The word 'button' derives from the French *'bouton'*, which in turn comes from the verb meaning 'to push'. This would imply that any type of fastener, such as a toggle which is pushed through fabric, should qualify as a button. However, in the accepted sense of the word, a button is taken to mean any flat object, usually round, that is used as a fastener in this way.

The earliest use of buttons is very difficult to establish, but as far as Britain is concerned, the first examples are probably of Bronze Age date. Perforated discs of bone and shale exist, as do gold cones which probably covered wooden or bone buttons. It is always possible that these may have been decorative mounts, but their overall form certainly strongly suggests that they were used as buttons.

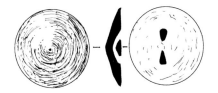

Shale button of Bronze Age date

Various types of toggle and loop fastener are known from both Iron Age and Roman times, although actual buttons are much more difficult to identify. Bronze buttons are illustrated in a few excavation reports, but are so much like medieval and later types as to cast some doubt on the accuracy of the dating. Button-like fastenings can however be seen on certain statues of the Roman period, so they may well have enjoyed at least a brief popularity on certain types of garment, although no specifically Roman style of button has yet been identified.

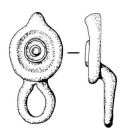

Button-and-loop fastener of late Iron Age or early Roman period date.

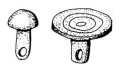

Bronze buttons attributed to the Roman period. From Germany.

There is little evidence for the use of buttons during the Saxon period, but they were certainly used by the Vikings, who in the 10th century AD adopted the wearing of buttoned kaftans. These spread to Scandinavia from the Eastern Caliphates via Russia. They are of very similar style to later medieval examples, and so chance finds of this early period could be incorrectly attributed.

Bronze button from a 10th century Swedish burial.

By the later Middle Ages, sculpture and illustrations show that for certain fashions at least, buttons were being used. The effigy of Casimir III of Poland in Cracow Cathedral (*circa* 1370) depicts the monarch wearing a tunic with a row of some thirteen or more large dished buttons secured through button holes. There are also written sources that provide evidence for their use in the 13th and 14th centuries, although securely dated specimens seem elusive. The advent of the cote-hardie in the 14th century required the use of many buttons, although these could have been made from fabric rather than metal. An early method of making buttons was by sewing a small piece of cloth into a tight ball, and such buttons have been recovered from medieval as well as later contexts. More positive dating evidence certainly exists for metal buttons in the 14th and 15th centuries however, and a number of examples from relatively secure contexts have now been recorded.

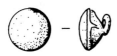

Lead alloy button from a 14th century context.

Brass button from a 14th - 15th century context.

Fashions of the Tudor and Stuart periods involved the use of buttons in great numbers. They were not only used for fastening, but also for decorative purposes and appear on contemporary portraits in runs along tunics, and down sleeves etc. There are many contemporary references in wills and inventories that refer to buttons made of gold and silver, or set with precious stones, although few examples seem to have survived. Given that gold and silver jewellery items such as rings and brooches are not uncommon metal detector finds, it seems odd that easily lost items such as buttons remain elusive. It is possible that many of the gold and silver buttons referred to were made of braid rather than solid metal, and thus, although their use could have been widespread, such buttons would be unlikely to survive to this day. The London Guild of Gold and Silver Wyre Drawers can trace its origins to craftsmen of the 15th century, and it is possible that the braid they produced may have been used for buttons as well as for other decorative purposes. It may be significant that the wreck of the *Mary Rose* produced only a few fabric buttons, and no metal buttons that could be securely attributed to the date of the loss of the ship (1545). If the crew of the ship can be taken as a reasonable cross-section of Tudor male society, military, marine and civilian, and if all buttons found were recorded, this implies that button use was very limited on everyday costume.

Metal buttons attributed to the 16th - 17th centuries

Metal buttons seem to become more prolific from the beginning of the 17th century, and a number of securely dated examples are known. Whilst one must be mindful of the fact that old buttons may be reused on later clothes, or that old clothes may acquire new buttons, it is apparent that small globular metal buttons were being used from at least 1600. A number of such buttons were found, securely stratified, on the Swedish warship *Vasa* (lost 1628). Typically, they comprised either spherical tin buttons with separately applied wire shanks, or one-piece castings with long shanks. They seem to have been employed on specific garments, possibly doublets. Shoes it seems were fastened with wooden pegs, boots were pull-on and did not have buttons. No large flat buttons for coats were noted, but many wire hooks and eyes were present. Further evidence for metal globular buttons of this period comes from a jacket in Rotterdam Museum dated to 1621, and from a Colonial period site at Wolstenholme in North America which was destroyed by Native Americans in 1622.

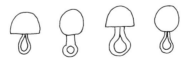

Profiles of buttons recovered from the Vasa

Following the Restoration of 1662, fashion became increasingly flamboyant, and the use of buttons, functional and decorative, proliferated. Inventories refer to gold and silk buttons, perhaps meaning an incorporation of gold braid with silk. An early 18th century advertisement refers to a coat with gold buttons and gold button holes, again suggesting the use of braid rather than solid metal.

Until the early 1700's, button manufacture was largely a cottage industry. The cast metal types referred to previously were probably the product of specific European centres, but many fabric buttons were very localised industries. Lace from

Buckinghamshire, silk from the West Midlands, linen 'Dorset' buttons from that county. When in the early 1700's it became fashionable to have buttons covered with the same material as that of the garment, riots occurred amongst traditional button makers who saw their livelihoods threatened.

Early buttons seem to have been predominately one-piece castings with either an integral shank, or an embedded wire one. From the latter part of 17th century hollow globular buttons were made, which characteristically have an internally secured shank and one or two small holes to allow expanding gases to escape when the two halves were soldered together.

The Industrial Revolution provided the means of producing quantities of metal buttons at affordable prices, and from the mid 18th century large decorative buttons became commonplace. These were mainly intended for the male fashions of the period, and included buttons of Wedgwood pottery, enamelled buttons, buttons that incorporated painted miniatures, gilded brass and copper examples, and cut steel varieties.

The early part of the 19th century saw a trend towards smaller and plainer buttons for men, but female fashion moved towards fitted garments that required numerous buttons, leading to a new upsurge in decorative button production. All manner of materials were employed, glass being particularly popular. Papier-mâché, horn and tortoiseshell were used, along with more exotic materials such as carved ivory, cinnabar and Italian mosaic. Japanese Satsuma Ware buttons were also imported. Decorative buttons on male dress were normally confined to waistcoats, picture buttons being particularly popular in the late Victorian/Edwardian eras. Outdoor coat buttons with hunting and shooting themes were also much in vogue. Two-piece buttons with separate backs were produced from the late 18th century.

Until the late 19th century, most decorative buttons were attached to garments with clips or split pins. This allowed them to be removed when clothing was washed. As the 20th century progressed, particularly following the First World War, the demand for less labour-intensive domestic activities led to sew-on buttons of simple style being produced, which could be left on a garment when it was laundered.

One reaction to the trend towards cheap mass production was the development of the Arts and Crafts movement, which led to buttons being produced by Moorcrofts, Pilkington and Ruskins. Art Nouveau and Art Deco styles proliferated, and materials such a celluloid were used for buttons to simulate more expensive substances. The Second World War brought great material shortages, leading to buttons being made from painted wood and plastic.

The post-war years saw the growing use of plastics in button manufacture, with metallic finishes becoming popular and negating the need to match buttons to the fabric of a garment. By the end of the 20th century, zippers, press-studs and velcro have largely replaced buttons for many applications, and buttons have become relatively scarce items on clothing, although those that are used may often have a designer or brand name on them.

2.

ARMED FORCES BUTTONS

The British Army

In 1767, an order was issued requiring regimental numbers to be placed on the uniform buttons of officers and other ranks. Prior to this order, military buttons were of an ornamental or plain functional nature. Officers wore gilt or silvered buttons, other ranks ones of pewter. Early military buttons are of a flat profile, but from about 1800 those worn by officers tended to be convex and open-backed, closed-backs being introduced during the 1820's. Other ranks continued to wear pewter buttons until 1855 when the tunic was introduced, and with it a larger size button, in gilt for officers, and brass for other ranks. In 1830, silvered buttons for regular regiments were replaced with gilt, with only the militia continuing to wear silvered buttons. In 1871, albeit with the exception of a few regiments and corps, a General Service button bearing the Royal Arms was issued for all other ranks. These continued to be used until 1924 when regimental buttons were reintroduced. In 1881, the Army was reorganised, and eighty-three numbered infantry regiments became the 1st and 2nd battalions of forty-one new named regiments. In consequence, numbered buttons were replaced with new types bearing regimental designations or crests. Military buttons made from aluminium were used by other European countries from the early part of the 20th century, but anodised aluminium was only adopted by the British in the early 1950's.

British military buttons form a complex subject, and reflect several different periods of army structuring, and involve numerous corps and volunteer forces. Over the years, many regiments were disbanded and reformed, or were amalgamated, and thus the dating of specific regimental buttons will also be dependant on such historical considerations as well as overall style. The regiments of the British Army comprise infantry and cavalry, supported by various corps. Additionally, there have also been volunteer forces raised at times of crises, of which some had specific types of button. The 1757 Militia Act formalised the establishment of a force raised by ballot, which was to act as a home defence unit. The militias became the 3rd battalions of the county regiments, and continued until 1908 when the Militia was replaced by the Territorial Force. Distinct from the Militia were the Volunteers, raised in 1794, and dissolved in 1813. Another volunteer force with different terms of service was the Local Militia. This body was instigated in 1800, and lasted only until 1816. Many small local militias were raised, and their uniform buttons are often extremely rare. In 1859 another force of volunteers was created, and this continued like the Militia until the formation of the Territorial Force. In the early 19th century mounted yeomanry volunteers were raised, and these remained as a distinct type of unit until their amalgamation into the Territorials in 1921, although unlike the Rifle Volunteers they continued to use their own buttons.

Infantry of the Line before 1881.

Most pre-1881 Infantry of the Line buttons feature the regimental number prominently displayed. Scottish regiments sometimes employed diamond-shaped doublet buttons.

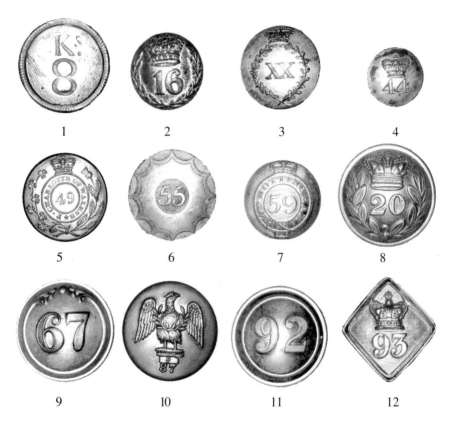

1. *The 8th King's Regt. Other ranks' pewter c1780-1800.*
2. *The 16th (Bedfordshire) Regt. Other rank's pewter c1800-1855.*
3. *The 20th (E. Devonshire) Regt. Officers' silvered c1800-1830.*
4. *The 44th (E. Essex) Regt. Officers' silvered c1800-1830.*
5. *The 49th (Hertfordshire) Regt. Officers' gilt 1816-1855.*
6. *The 55th (Westmorland) Regt. Officers' gilt c1800-1830.*
7. *The 59th (2nd Notts) Regt. Officers' gilt 1830-1855.*
8. *The 20th (E. Devonshire) Regt. 1855-1881.*
9. *The 67th (S. Hants) Regt. 1855-1881.*
10. *The 87th (PoW Own Irish Fusiliers) 1855-1881.*
11. *The 92nd (Gordon Highlanders) 1855-1881.*
12. *The 93rd (Sutherland Highlanders) Officers' gilt doublet button 1855-1856.*

Infantry of the Line after 1881

After 1881, the regimental number was replaced by regimental crests and motifs. Some have a legend giving the regiment's name, whilst others do not.

1. *The Beds & Herts Regt. 1919-1958.*
2. *The Essex Regt. 1902 - 1958.*
3. *The Border Regt. 1884-1959.*
4. *The King's (Liverpool) Regt. 1920-1958.*
5. *The Gordon Highlanders. 1881 onwards.*
6. *The Lincolnshire Regt. 1881-1946.*
7. *The Queen's Lancashire Regt. 1979 onwards.*
8. *The Queen's Own Royal West Kent Regt. 1881-1959.*
9. *The Somerset Light Infantry. 1881-1959.*

Volunteers and Militia

As with buttons of the regular army, early volunteer and militia buttons are one-piece, flat or concave. Later ones are two-piece, with larger buttons for the 1855 tunic. Most buttons either have the words 'Militia' or 'Volunteers' on them, or initials including 'M' or 'V'. Some early units styled themselves 'Fencibles'. Some buttons have a number similar to the regular infantry, but usually with some other legend to indicate that the unit is not a Regiment of the Line.

1. *1st. Hertfordshire Volunteers. c1800.*
2. *Andover Loyal Volunteers. c1800.*
3. *4th. Royal Lancashire Militia. Pre-1855.*
4. *4th Aberdeenshire Local Militia. 1800-1816.*
5. *Westmorland (E&W Wards) Local Militia. 1800-1816.*
6. *Newton & Falsworth Local Militia. 1800-1816.*
7. *Royal N. Gloucestershire Militia. 1855-1881.*
8 *Hertfordshire Militia. 1855-1881.*
9. *1st. Lancashire Volunteer Rifles. 1859-1908.*
10. *1st Hants Volunteer Artillery. 1860-1908.*
11. *London Irish Rifle Volunteers. 1914-1936.*
12. *28th County of London (Territorial) Battalion - The Artists' Rifles. 1914-1936.*

Cavalry and Yeomanry

Regular cavalry buttons often have initials such as 'L.G.' for Life Guards, 'D.G.' for Dragoon Guards, 'L.D.' for Light Dragoons, 'H' for Hussars, or combinations of initials in script. Lancers' buttons usually depict lances with pennants. Yeomanry may have the unit name, or initials sometimes including a 'Y' for Yeomanry. Some 20th century cavalry buttons are engraved flat gilt, and look much earlier than they really are.

1. *1st. Life Guards. Officer's gilt. c1850.*
2. *Royal Horse Guards. Until 1969.*
3. *5th Dragoon Guards. Officer's gilt 1840-1855.*
4. *4th/7th Dragoon Guards. 1922 onwards.*
5. *11th. Hussars. Pre-1940.*
6. *6th Dragoon Guards (Carabiniers). c1850-1870.*
7. *14/20th King's Hussars. After 1920.*
8. *12th Royal Lancers. c1851-1960.*
9. *Loyal Lincolnshire Yeomanry. Flat gilt. c1800-1830.*
10. *Essex Imperial Yeomanry. 1855 onwards.*
11. *Berkshire Yeomanry. Until 1956.*
12. *Earl of Chester's Yeomanry. 1907-1950's.*

Corps and Miscellaneous

Just as there are many hundreds of different buttons for the various types of infantry and cavalry forces, equally numerous are those of the corps and support services that have made up the British Army over the years. The following are a small sample of that diversity.

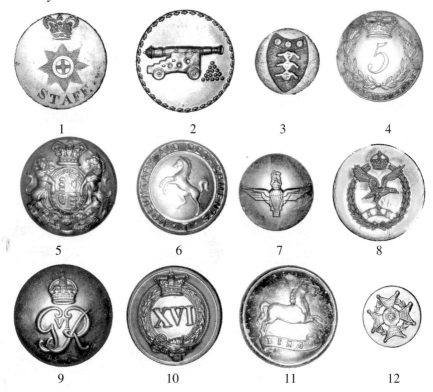

1. *Staff Officer. Gilt c1800.*
2. *Royal Regt. of Artillery. Gilt with bone back. 1767-1785.*
3. *Royal Regt. of Artillery. Pewter c1800.*
4. *5th Royal Veterans Corps. 1804-1815.*
5. *General Service button 1871-1901 (Queen's crown).*
6. *Voluntary Aid Detachment. 1914-1920.*
7. *The Parachute Regt. 1940's onwards.*
8. *Army Air Corps. 1942-1950.*
9. *Royal Military Police. 1937-1952.*
10. *Bedfordshire Regt. Mess staff.*
11. *The Kings Regt. (Liverpool). Mess staff.*
12. *The Border Regt. Officers' Mess dress button.*

Navy and Air Force

Naval buttons of the 18th and early 19th centuries were flat with a simple anchor motif. Later examples become two-piece, and have a King's or Queen's crown over the anchor and a rope edge. Some variations denote different rank. Admirals' buttons have a wreath around the anchor. Branches such as Fisheries Protection and the Royal Naval Volunteer Reserve incorporate a legend or initials into the anchor design. Naval aviation came under the aegis of the Royal Naval Air Service, which together with the Royal Flying Corps was amalgamated into the Royal Air Force in 1918. The Royal Navy again assumed control of naval flying in 1938, with the formation of the Fleet Air Arm.

The Royal Flying Corps was created in 1912 from the Army Air Battalion. During the First World War, aircraft manufacture was carried out at Farnborough at the Royal Aircraft Factory, and buttons of that establishment bear the letters 'RAF'. This has no connection with the later Royal Air Force. The only design change to the Royal Air Force button since its establishment has been from a King's to a Queen's crown in 1952.

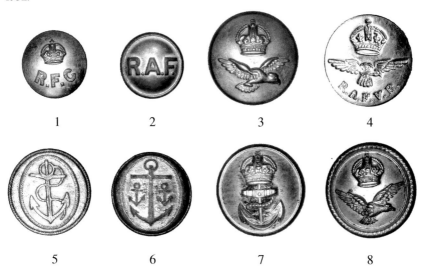

1. *Royal Flying Corps. 1912-1918.*
2. *Royal Aircraft Factory. 1914-1918.*
3. *Royal Air Force. 1918-1952.*
4. *Royal Air Force Volunteer Reserve. Blazer button*
5. *Royal Navy. Captain 1795-1812.*
6. *Royal Navy. Master 1825.*
7. *Royal Navy. King's crown.*
8. *Fleet Air Arm. WW2 period.*

3.

CIVILIAN UNIFORM BUTTONS

Uniforms are worn by a wide range of civilian organizations, of which a majority are fitted with their own distinctive buttons. National organisations such as the Post Office usually have a royal crown in the design. Emergency services frequently employ town, borough or county arms or crests.

Transport companies usually provided their employees with uniform buttons. The earliest were mail coach crew who wore heavy overcoats as protection against extreme weather. Consequently their buttons tend to be very large with an elongated shank. Both tram and omnibus companies used their own buttons. Prior to 1923, there was a vast network of different railway companies. Some company buttons have emblems or early locomotives in the design - the date of the engine does not denote the age of the buttons however - many used an early locomotive on buttons up until 1923! Other companies' buttons are simply initials, usually ending in 'R'. From 1923 until 1948 the railway companies were grouped into four, the London Midland & Scottish, the London North Eastern, the Great Western and the Southern Railway. These in turn were nationalised into British Railways in 1948.

Shipping buttons are a large category, the majority having a rope edge design. They can be distinguished from Royal Naval types by either having a company name or initials, or a houseflag. Marine services include docks and harbour boards, pilots, Trinity House, HM Customs, Coast Guards and even canals and other inland waterways.

Sailing clubs are very fond of quality buttons comparable to those of early shipping companies. A large proportion have the "Royal ---Yacht Club" (or initials) under a Victorian crown plus an anchor. This does not necessarily date the button to the 19th century however, as the crown denotes when the club became 'Royal'.

Many other types of sporting club had their own buttons, particularly rowing and golfing clubs. Other sporting clubs may include athletics, cricket, rugby, soccer, hockey and archery.

Commercial companies often had livery buttons for various employees, ranging from doormen to drivers. Victorian ones are often of high quality and impressive appearance, as companies vied with each other for prestige. The Victorian Age also saw the establishment of many hospitals and mental institutions, which employed large numbers of uniformed attendants and porters. The word 'Asylum' was replaced by 'Mental Hospital' after 1930. The introduction of the school blazer led to a huge range of buttons with crests and school mottoes.

Livery buttons were produced by civic organisations and masonic lodges, and some of the London livery companies have their own. Private livery buttons form a distinct class, produced for the domestic staff of wealthy families. These frequently bear coats of arms, family crests, or noble coronets, down to various designs used by non-titled families.

Emergency Services - Police

1   2   3

1. St. Austell Police. By Firmin & Son. Silver on copper. Pre-1879.
2. Lancashire Police. By J. & B. Pearse & Son. White metal. Victorian.
3. Maidstone Police. By J. Compton Sons & Webb Ltd. White metal. Early 20th century.

Emergency Services - Fire Brigades

1   2   3   4

1. Ross-on-Wye Fire Brigade. One-piece gilt. By Jennens & Co. c1900.
2. Borough of Margate. Two-piece brass. By Firmin & Sons. Victorian.
3. Oxford Voluntary Maintained Fire Brigade. No backmark. Early 20th century
4. National Fire Service. Second World War.

Public Services - Post Office

1   2

1. General Post Office. Stamped with number of letter carrier. One-piece brass c1800.
2. General Post Office. Two-piece brass. By Harrison & Smith. Victorian.

Transport - Coaches

                    1   2

1. Coachman's button. Silver on copper. Legend 'We push along with four in hand'.
2. Back of previous. By Hammond, Turner & Sons. Georgian crown. c1820.

Transport - Trams.

          1   2   3

1. Birkenhead Street Railway Co. One-piece brass. 1860-1876.
2. Newcastle Corporation Tramway. White metal.
3. Bristol Tramway & Carriage Co. Ltd. White metal.

Transport - Omnibuses.

              1   2

1. General Omnibus Co. (now part of London Transport). White metal. 1930's.
2. Southport Corporation Transport. Chrome on brass. c1950.

Transport - Breakdown Services

1   2

1. *Automobile Association. Plastic.*
2. *Royal Automobile Club. Chrome.*

Transport - Railways

Backmarks for J. Compton & Son, Webb & Co., or Smith & Wright frequently indicate railway buttons.

1. *Great Western & Midland Railway (joint line). Senior staff. Gilt. Late Victorian.*
2. *Somerset & Dorset Joint Committee. White metal. Style used 1875-1930.*
3. *Aylesbury Joint Station. Brass.*
4. *Brecon & Merthyr Railway. Brass for senior staff. 1863-1923.*
5. *Great Western Railway. 1934-1948 design.*
6. *Caledonian Station Hotel, Edinburgh. Two-piece brass.*

Transport - Shipping and Marine Services

Many shipping buttons have the backmark of marine tailors such as Miller, Rayner & Haysom Ltd.

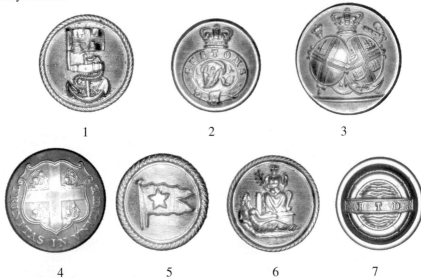

1   2   3

4   5   6   7

1. *Richard Green Line. By Goy & Co. Backmark for 1861-1876.*
2. *H.M. Customs. By Hibbert & Co. Late Victorian.*
3. *Thames Conservancy. Brass one-piece. By J. Compton. Late Victorian.*
4. *Trinity House. One piece.*
5. *White Star Line. By F. Stillwell & Son. Early 20th century.*
6. *Mersey Docks & Harbour Board. By JSM & Co. 1930's.*
7. *British Transport Docks. Chrome. By Firmin. 1950's.*

Transport - Airlines

1   2   3

1. *Chart Air. By Firmin.*
2. *Imperial Airways. By Miller, Rayner & Haysom Ltd.*
3. *British Overseas Airways Corporation (BOAC). By Gaunt.*

Commerce and Industry

1. *Yeovil Agricultural Society. Brass one-piece. By MS&JD. Mid 19th century.*
2. *Cavendish Club London. One-piece wrapped edge. By Firmin. Early 20th century.*
3. *Sun Insurance. White metal. By C&J Weldon. Early 20th century.*
4. *Imperial Hotel. By Firmin & Son. Mid-Victorian.*
5. *Hyde Park Hotel. Brass wrapped edge. By Firmin & Sons Ltd. c1900.*
6. *London County & Westminster Bank Ltd. One-piece. By Pitt & Co. 1909-1918.*
7. *The Law Society. Brass, wrapped edge. By Firmin & Sons Ltd. c1900.*
8. *London Zoological Society. Two-piece brass.*
9. *Cheltenham Old Brewery. One-piece brass. c1900.*
10. *Esso. Driver's overall button. Two-piece.*
11. *Thomas & Evans (Corona Drinks). By Buttons Ltd. Chrome c1950.*
12. *Gaumont Cinemas. Commissionaire's button. By Gaunt. 1950's.*

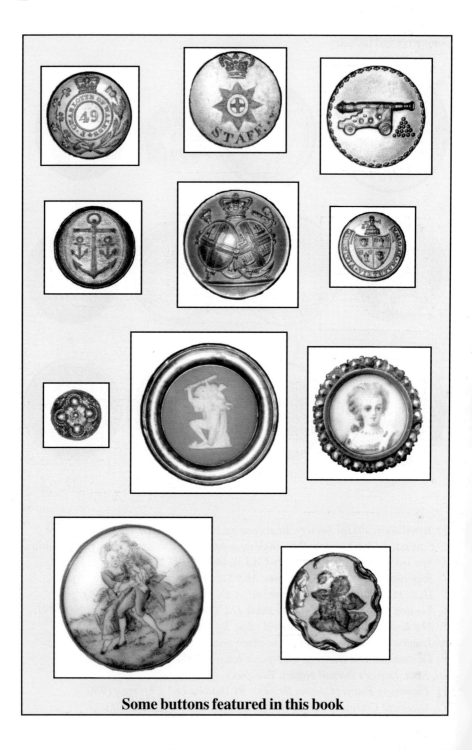

Some buttons featured in this book

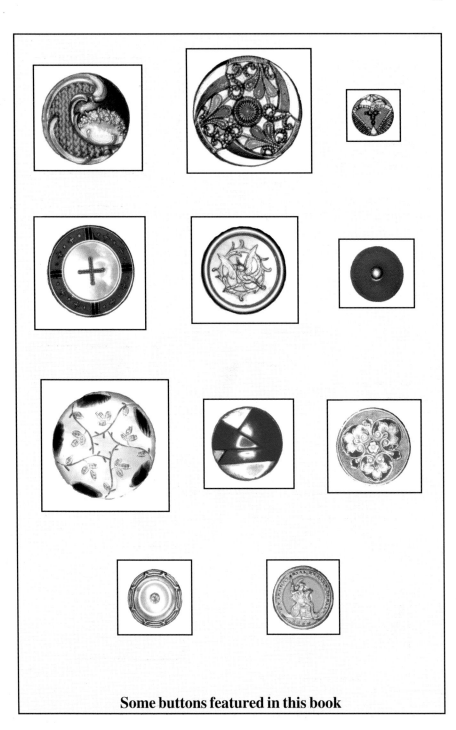

Some buttons featured in this book

Public Utilities

1. Birmingham Water Works Company. Flat two-piece. Early 19th century.
2. Metropolitan Water Board. Brass. No backmark.
3. North-West Electricity Board. Chrome.

Education and Medical

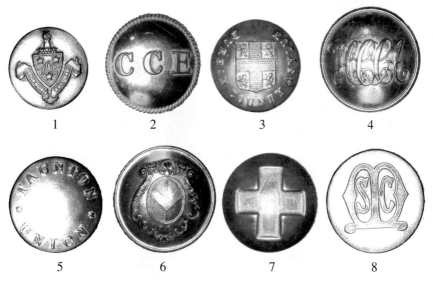

1. *Alleyns School, Dulwich College. One-piece blazer.*
2. *College of Civil Engineers. One-piece brass. By Firmin. c1840.*
3. *Durham County Asylum. One-piece brass. Early 20th century.*
4. *Herefordshire County Council Asylum. One-piece. By Firmin. Pre-1930.*
5. *Taunton Parish Union Workhouse. Silvered brass. Early 19th century.*
6. *St. Bartholomews Hospital, London. One-piece. Late 19th/early 20th century.*
7. *Early Red Cross. Incuse motif. Two-piece brass.*
8. *State Certified Midwives. 1946-1966.*

Sporting Clubs

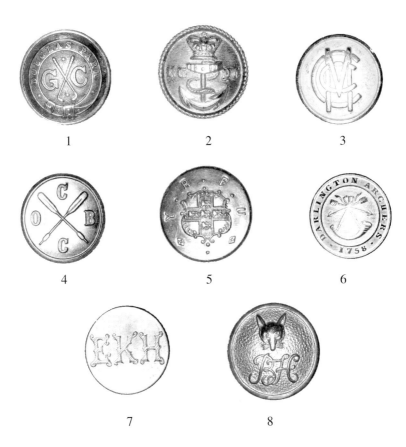

1. *Douglas Park Golf Club. Silver, hallmarked 1920.*
2. *Royal Thames Yacht Club.*
3. *Marylebone Cricket Club.*
4. *Oakley College Boating Club.*
5. *York Rugby Union Football Club.*
6. *Darlington Archery Club.*
7. *East Kent Hunt. Brass one-piece. Etched.*
8. *Bisley Hunt. Brass one-piece.*

Livery Buttons

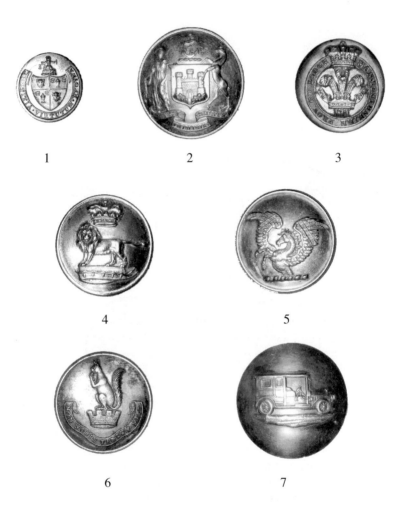

1. *City livery. The Goldsmiths' Company.*
2. *Civic livery. Edinburgh City. By Kirkwood.*
3. *Masonic livery. Provincial Grand Lodge Monmouthshire. Victorian.*
4. *Household livery. The Duke of Norfolk. By Jennens.*
5. *Household livery. Crest of Trafford. One-piece white metal. Mid Victorian.*
6. *Household livery. Crest of Warner. One piece silver on copper. Mid Victorian.*
7. *Household livery. Chauffeur's button. By Firmin & Sons Ltd. Early 20th century.*

4.

DECORATIVE AND UTILITARIAN BUTTONS

The scope encompassed by non-uniform buttons is vast, but nonetheless it is possible to classify decorative and utilitarian buttons to a reasonable extent. Many designations are simply descriptive, but other terms have grown up amongst button collectors, and are now generally used.

Very few buttons of gold are known, and it is doubtful if they saw wide usage. Those that are known were probably only clipped onto a garment when required and worn for special occasions. Gilt buttons are however frequently encountered. The 'dandy' of the 18th century wore many large flat buttons on his coat, gilded examples being popular. In order to prevent fraud, an Act of Parliament of 1796 stipulated that gilded buttons were to be so marked. In consequence, many gilt buttons will be encountered with back stamps such as 'double gilt' or 'triple gilt' (the number of times a button was dipped in the plating amalgam), 'superfine', 'extra fine' and other such slogans. Collectors refer to these types as 'Golden Age' buttons. Such legends were not always a guarantee of quality however, and some buttons were produced using a poor quality dip known as 'dandelion water'.

Silver has been widely used for buttons, in either solid, sheet or plated form. Small globular silver buttons seem to be common metal detector finds. These have copper-alloy loops inset into them. So far they have not been dated satisfactorily, but on stylistic grounds they seem likely to be of 16th or 17th century date and were probably of a decorative nature. Other spherical sheet silver buttons have makers' marks of 17th and 18th century type. Flat silver buttons with engraved fronts were produced in the 18th and 19th centuries, and more recently in various styles. Recent ones of British origin will be hallmarked. Silver-plated buttons occur from the mid-eighteenth century in many forms ranging from plain to decorative and livery.

Cut steel became a popular medium for button manufacture, deriving from a craft developed in Oxfordshire in the late 17th century. Early Woodstock steels have individual threaded studs which were screwed into the button plate. By the late 18th century Birmingham manufacturers were producing similar buttons with riveted studs, and this style became part of the standard Court Dress still in use today. By the mid 19th century cut steel buttons were being imitated by producing silver-washed sheet metal fronts mounted on a button back. 20th century "steels" tend to be of one-piece moulded design made from a variety of materials, predominately lustred glass.

Tin and pewter has been used for buttons from the 17th century, plain or engraved pewter being a cheaper alternative to silver or silver-plated examples. Tin was widely used in the 19th and 20th centuries for mass-produced stamped buttons.

Many early buttons were made from copper-alloy; possibly some may have been gilded. Copper was used during the eighteenth century for male coat buttons, but this was superseded by brass and similar alloys, which were often gilded or silvered. Some early brass buttons were produced by overlaying a sheet of brass on a bone back, which was secured by crossed catgut.

Glass, papier-mâché, woven linen, wood, shell, pressed clay, bone and plastic are amongst other materials used for specific decorative or utilitarian purposes.

Pictorial buttons were produced in the 18th and 19th centuries which were hand painted on porcelain or ivory. Later examples used lithographs under celluloid. Edwardian gentlemen wore pictorial buttons on their waistcoats, a style revived for advertising purposes in the 1950's.

Enamelling was employed on decorative buttons of the 19th and 20th centuries, pearl and tortoiseshell also being used to great effect. Such buttons border on fine art, and are referred to as "Collectors' Treasures".

Buttons have been used as commemorative souvenirs for various events. They have also been made from coins, and made to imitate coins. They have been made to imitate military or marine buttons for modern fashion clothing, or for sporting clothes such as yachting blazers etc.

At the plain utilitarian end of the subject, bone, linen and pearl were widely employed for shirts and under garments, plastic replacing them in the 20th century. Braces and overalls were fitted with dished brass buttons often stamped with the name of the clothing retailer.

Note: The use of cuff-links grew from the late 17th century onwards, and some round examples may be confused with buttons when found singly. Likewise large double-link cloak fasteners were used. A few are included in the following selection for comparison.

Gold and Gilded Buttons

1

2   3

1. Gold button. Hollow spherical construction with applied decoration and engraved floral motifs. No maker's mark or hallmark. Probably late 17th century.

2. Typical backmark of an early 19th century gilt button.

3. Gilt brass with hand-tooled decoration. No backmark. 18th/19th centuries.

Gold and gilded buttons (continued).

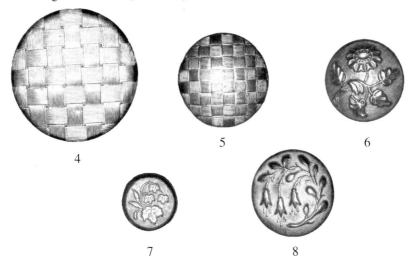

4

5

6

7

8

4. *Gilt 'dandy' button with weave pattern. No backmark. Late 18th century.*
5. *Similar gilt button of later date - a pattern still in use.*
6. *Gilt button c. 1820. Backmark 'Extra Treble Standd.'*
7. *Gilt decorative button, backmark 'Superfine Quality'. 19th century.*
8. *Poor quality 'dandelion water' button. Backmark 'Extra Superior Quality'. 19th century.*

Silver Buttons

1

2

3

4

1. *Globular buttons with inset brass loop. c16th/17th century.*
2. *Cuff-link. Crowned hearts die-stamped type. c17th/18th century. This type may be a reference to the marriage of Charles II and Catherine of Braganza.*
3. *Cuff-link. Die-stamped decorative type showing shank. c17th/18th century.*
4. *Globular hollow type with 'IH' (or 'HI') maker's mark in cartouche. c17th/18th century.*

Silver buttons (continued).

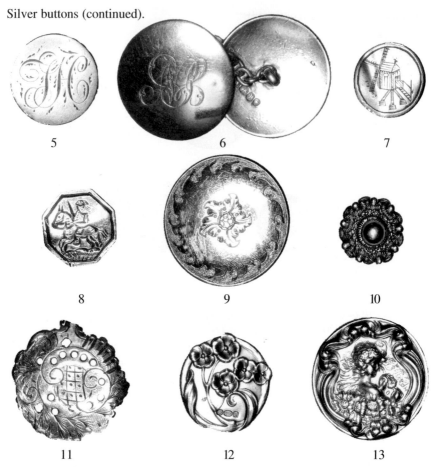

5

6

7

8

9

10

11

12

13

5. *Engraved initials. Reverse with maker's mark for Bateman, hallmarked 1810.*
6. *Engraved initials. Double button cloak-fastener. By Firmin, hallmarked for
    1826.*
7. *Dutch made traditional design. 19th century.*
8. *Dutch made depicting William of Orange. Maker's mark 'I.G.' in cartouche on
    back. Despite the early look, these buttons are 19th century.*
9. *Decorative type with maker's mark of Thomas Teale and hallmarked for 1739 on
    the back. The edging is contemporary but the centre motif was added in
    Victorian times.*
10. *Spherical ornate type. The rear half openwork. 19th century*
11. *Handworked type. Backmark 'S+Co' and hallmarked for 1900.*
12. *Front-marked decorative French import. 'RF' mark, sunface mark, .925 silver
    mark and 'K' mark for London 1905.*
13. *Art Nouveau style. Hallmarked Birmingham 1905.*

Cut Steel Buttons

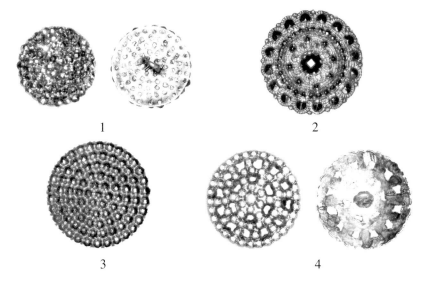

1

2

3

4

1. Cut steel button with individual cut and polished rivets set onto a brass disc. 18th century.
2. Court Dress button. Traditional pattern.
3. Glass imitating cut steel. 19th century.
4. One-piece moulded alloy - no rivets. 20th century.

Decorative, Pictorial and Patterned Buttons

1

2

1. Wedgewood cameo set in copper. 1780's.
2. Hand painted on ivory. Marcasite edge. Georgian.

Decorative, Pictorial and Patterned Buttons (continued).

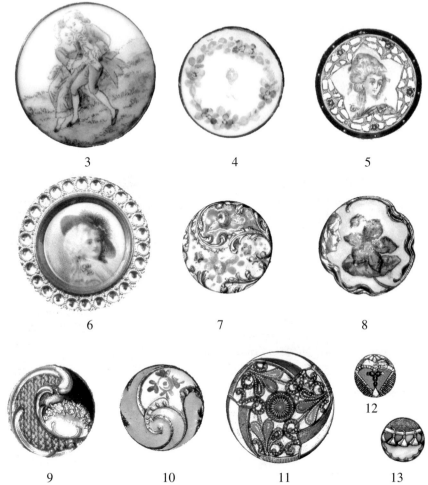

3   4   5

6   7   8

9   10   11   12   13

3. *Hand painted porcelain in brass. Victorian.*
4. *Hand painted porcelain. 19th century.*
5. *Hand painted on enamel. Victorian.*
6. *Lithograph under celluloid with imitation cut steel edge. Late 19th/early 20th*
   century.
7. *Hand painted champlevé enamel. c1900.*
8. *Hand painted enamel. Art Nouveau.*
9. *Painted metal with fabric insert. Art Nouveau.*
10.*'Cold enamel' painted on brass.*
11. *Painted tin. Czech made 1930's.*
12. *and 13. Composite small decoratives. 'Austrian tinies'. c1880-1900.*

Decorative, Pictorial and Patterned Buttons (continued).

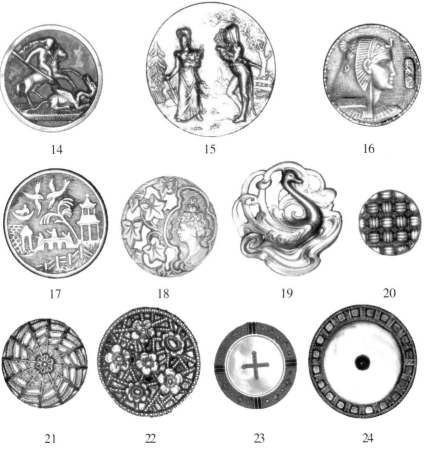

14   15   16

17   18   19   20

21   22   23   24

14. George & Dragon. Patriotic picture button inspired by Queen Victoria's 1897 Jubilee.

15. Paris made c1880 evoking French Revolutionary fashions.

16. Egyptian motifs inspired by 20th century archaeological discoveries.

17. Chinese 'Willow Pattern'. Pressed brass. 19th century.

18. Stamped brass Art Nouveau style.

19. Stamped brass Art Nouveau style.

20. One-piece brass weave pattern. Backmark 'T.W.& W. HM. Paris Brevete'. Late 19th/early 20th century.

21. Fretted metal over tin. Backmark 'Made in Czechoslovakia'. 1930's.

22. One-piece decorative. Post-World War Two style.

23. Pearl set in brass with enamel edge. Edwardian.

24. Metal back with pearl disc attached. Post-World War Two.

Decorative, Pictorial and Patterned Buttons (continued).

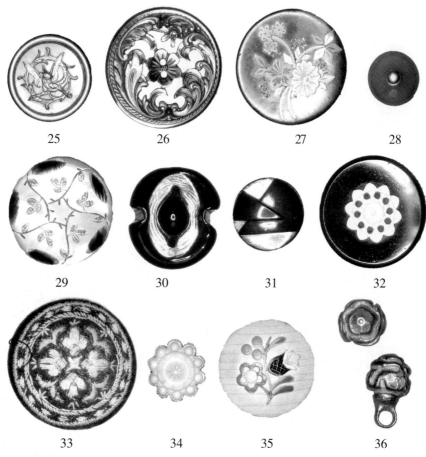

25   26   27   28

29   30   31   32

33   34   35   36

25. *Dragon escutcheon on pearl mounted in brass. c1900.*
26. *Carved grey pearl with metal decoration. Victorian.*
27. *Tortoiseshell on horn, with gold silver and pearl inlay. Early Victorian.*
28. *Cornelian with metal pin shank. c1900.*
29. *Abalone shell ovals set into an etched pearl base. Metal shank. Victorian.*
30. *Impressed glass. Backmark 'Bimini Ltd. Made in England'. 1940's-50's.*
31. *Silvered glass. Art Deco style.*
32. *Black glass with pearl escutcheon. Metal loop shank. Victorian.*
33. *Embroidered to match garment. Georgian. Later copies exist.*
34. *Carved bone with metal shank. Victorian.*
35. *Embossed and painted wood. c1930-1950's.*
36. *Chinese tunic button. Hand worked brass with loop for braid attachment. Pre-1900.*

Decorative, Pictorial and Patterned Buttons (continued).

| 37 | 38 | 39 | 40 | 41 |

37. Inlaid enamel in Indian silver. Backmark for Mohammedia Button Factory Deccan.
1935-1950's.

38. Gentleman's waistcoat. Green diamante set in pearl with silver plate mounts.
Edwardian.

39. Gentleman's waistcoat. Brass 'x' set in pearl. Edwardian.

40. Gentleman's waistcoat. Fox's head under glass. 1950's.

41. Gentleman's waistcoat. Guinness advertising motif. 1950's.

Commemorative Buttons

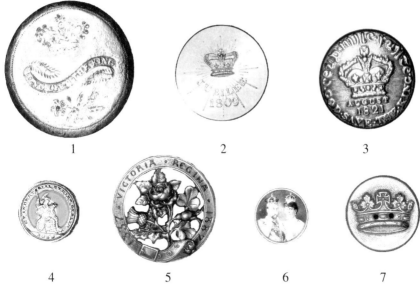

| 1 | 2 | 3 |
| 4 | 5 | 6 | 7 |

1. Struck c1789 on return of King's health and to show support in the face of the
French and American Revolutionary Movements.

2. One-piece button struck for the Jubilee of George III 1809.

3. Two-piece button to commemorate the visit of George IV to Ireland in 1821.

4. Gilt and enamel. The Great Industrial Exhibition, Dublin 1853.

5. Stamped and painted brass. Queen Victoria's Jubilee 1887.

6. Waistcoat button. The Coronation of George V 1911.

7. One of four buttons given with 'Women and Beauty' magazine as a Coronation
souvenir in 1937. The others depicted a thistle, a shamrock and a Tudor rose.

Coin Buttons

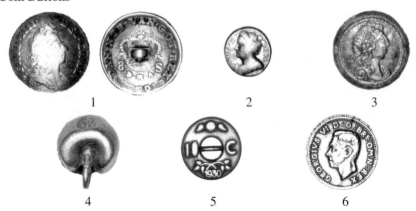

1   2   3

4   5   6

1. *Button made from a Norwegian silver 8 skilling coin of 1701. This issue was widely used for buttons and other jewellery purposes in Scandinavia..*
2. *Cuff-link. Silver die-stamped after a coin of Queen Anne. Early 18th century.*
3. *Button in the style of a Georgian coin (pre-1800).*
4. *Siamese silver 'baht', a punch-marked globular coin, fitted with a shank for use as a button. An issue of Rama IV (1851-1868).*
5. *Utilitarian button based on a French 10 centimes of 1930.*
6. *Plastic button imitating a sixpence of George VI.*

Sporting Buttons

1   2

3   4

1. *Pewter button with engraved stag. 18th century.*
2. *Two-piece button depicting a shooting scene. 19th century.*
3. *Two-piece button depicting a hunting dog and pups. 19th century.*
4. *One-piece button with tennis rackets motif. Kitemark on back for 1881.*

Imitative Buttons

1   2   3

1. *Metal fashion button imitating Royal Artillery type. 1960's.*
2. *Plastic pseudo-military fashion. Late 20th century.*
3. *Fashion button imitating livery types. Late 20th century.*

Utilitarian Buttons

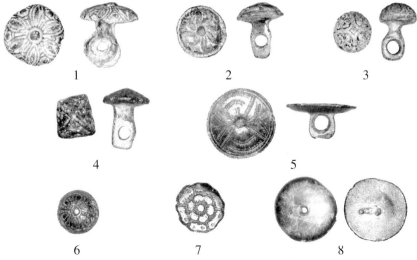

1   2   3

4   5

6   7   8

1. *Pewter one-piece. Integral long shank with decorated domed front. c16th/17th century.*
2. *Copper-alloy as previous.*
3. *Copper-alloy as previous.*
4. *As previous but with rectangular-shaped front.*
5. *Copper-alloy engraved front. Integral shank. c16th/17th century.*
6. *Pewter with decorated front. Wire inset shank (missing). c16th/17th century.*
7. *Pewter with front in form of a Tudor rose. Wire inset shank (missing). c16th/17th century.*
8. *Pewter. Domed with central nipple. Inset shank suggests an early date, although this style was used in Northern Europe until the 19th century.*

Utilitarian Buttons (continued).

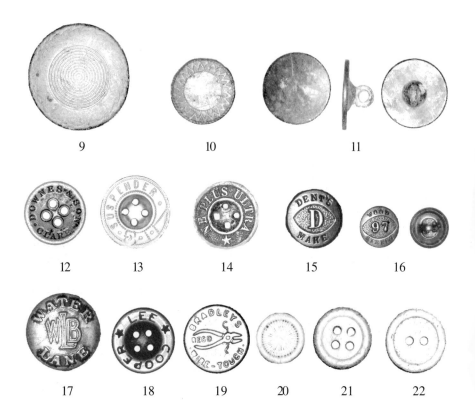

9. Flat pewter with decorated front. 18th/19th century.
10. Another smaller example.
11. Plain flat pewter with cone back. 18th/19th century. Many variations to this
     basic type can be found, with dished fronts, and slightly different forms of shank.
12. Overall or braces button. Local retailer's name. Late 19th/early 20th century.
13. Another marked 'suspender'.
14. Another marked 'Ne Plus Ultra'.
15. Glove button with name of manufacturer. 20th century.
16. Front and back of another glove button. Maker's address on front.
17. Overall button, Water Lane Brand. 20th century.
18. Lee Cooper jeans button. Late 20th century.
19. Overall button. Clip-on type for easier laundering. 20th century.
20. Dorset linen button. Type used from 17th to 19th century.
21. Bone four-hole button. Type used from 18th to 20th century.
22. As previous, two-hole variety.

Appendix 1
French Military Uniform Buttons
By Yann Ledru and David Smith.

In 1762, Louis XV decreed that military uniform buttons should bear a regimental number. The first ones had numbers applied to a wooden backing, with metal being used from 1767. Button sizes were 25mm for the campaign cloak, and 15mm for the tunic or waistcoat. The regimental number was enclosed in a circle, a design copied by the British. French military button-backs however differ in having a four-holed mount rather than a looped shank.

In 1792, the regimental numbers were replaced by a design incorporating the Cap of Liberty and the Fasces, with the revolutionary phrase 'Republique Française'. In 1793, to counter the threat of invasion, 'half-brigades' were raised. Their buttons had numbers in addition to the revolutionary symbols.

With the advent of Napoleon Bonaparte, the French Army burgeoned, and there is a corresponding increase in button variety. Button fronts now bore motifs such as an eagle for the Imperial Guard, crossed cannon for the Artillery, a hunting horn for the Light Infantry, and an anchor for the Navy. Others depicted the Spirit of the Republic wearing a breastplate.

From 1815, the previously flat buttons gave way to a slightly dished brass variety. Additionally, backmarks with the makers' names now appear. 'Cordier a Paris' is a common one. Officers' buttons were of a slightly greater diameter than those of other ranks.

After 1856, buttons became more domed, and have a longer cruciform shank. Regimental numbers and symbols remained unchanged.

The French Foreign Legion, founded in 1831, only received official distinction during the Second Empire (1852-70). Its buttons bear the legend 'Legion Étrangère' plus the numeral '1' or '2'. These buttons too were of brass.

From 1914, regimental numbers were replaced by a grenade symbol for the Infantry, crossed cannon for the Artillery, and a hunting horn for the Chasseurs.

1   2   3

1. Infantry button 1803-14
2. Imperial Guard. Napoleon III.
3. Infantry button of the 1914-18 period.

Appendix 2
Button Backmarks

Many of these can be more accurately dated by referring to differences in how the name of the company is presented (Ltd., partnerships etc.) and differing addresses.

Allen & Moore, Birmingham. 1855-70.
Armfield, Birmingham. 1763-1940's.
Bogget, London. 1824-61.
Broughton & Noakes, London. 1840-5.
Bushby, London. c1800-24.
Buttons Ltd. Birmingham. 1900's.
Cairns, Birmingham. c1795-1820.
Clancy, Dublin. 1817-47.
Firmin, London. 1763-1964.
Gaunt, Birmingham. 1870-1973.
Hammond Turner & etc., Birmingham. c1790-1955.
Hawkes, London. 1788-1890's.
Hobson, London. 1873-1890's.
Hunwick, London. 1853-55.
Jennens, London. c1800-1924.
Leonard, Birmingham. 1803-21.
Lucock, Birmingham. 1787-1835.
Nortzell & etc. 1825-38.
Nutting, London. c1800-1840.
Mann, Birmingham. c1800-1843.
Middleton, Littlewood & Co., Sheffield. c1800-10.
Moore, Birmingham. c1790-1825.
Pitt & etc., London. 1875-1973.
Reeves, London. 1853-1955.
Reynolds etc., London. 1861-73.
Sherlock, London. c1840-1887.
Smith, Kemp & Wright, Birmingham. c1845-1900's.
Starkey, London. 1835-1934.
Weldon, London. 1851-early 1900's.
Williams,I., London. 1791-1800.

Appendix 3
Kitemarks on Buttons

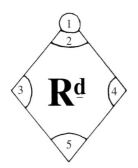

1842-1867
1. Numeral indicates material:
    I= Metal
    II= Wood
    III= Glass
    IV= Earthenware
    N= Horn
2. Letter indicates year of manufacture
3. Month letter
4. Day of month
5. Bundle or parcel number

Month letters in sequence for January to December: C,G,W,H,E,M,I,R,D,B,K,A.

Year letters in sequence for 1842 to 1867:
X,H,C,A,I,F,U,S,V,P,D,Y,J,E,L,K,B,M,Z,R,O,G,N,W,Q,T.

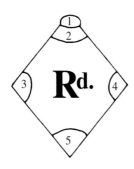

1868-1883
1. Numeral indicates material:
    I= Metal
    II= Wood
    III= Glass
    IV= Earthenware
    N= Horn
2. Day of month
3. Parcel number
4. Letter indicates year of manufacture
5. Month letter

Month letters as previous.

Year letters in sequence for 1868-1883:
X,H,C,A,I,F,U,S,V,P,D,Y,J,E,L,K.

Appendix 4
Crowns and Coronets found on Buttons

The different forms of crowns and coronets found on buttons can provide a guide to dating and identity. Three styles of royal crown were used on both service and some civilian uniform buttons. Different styles of coronet denote rank, and these may be used to assist in the identification of household livery buttons.

Crowns

1   2   3

1. George III to William IV.
2. Victoria and Elizabeth II.
3. Edward VII to George VI.

Coronets

1   2   3

4   5

1. Duke
2. Viscount
3. Marquis
4. Earl
5. Baron.

Appendix 5
Glossary of Button Terminology

Backmark: Legend or design on the reverse of a button.

Breveté: French term for patented.

Déposé: French term for registered trademark.

Golden Age: Gold-dipped button, late 18th to mid 19th century.

Kitemark: British Patent registration mark. (not BSI mark in button context).

Mounted: Design in escutcheon form attached to button.

One-piece: Single metal disc - domed or flat - with design on front and shank attached to back.

Paris Back: Button with Paris backmark. Not all were French-made, but the legend implied association with the home of haute couture.

Shank: Loop or mount for securing button to garment.

Two-piece: Domed metal disc carrying design - attached to flat disc carrying shank, leaving hollow centre.

Vest: US term for waistcoat.

Wrapped: Metal disc with shank attached, with top separate layer carrying design wrapped around it, leaving no hollow centre.

Bibliography

Baily's Hunting Directory. J. Allen & Co. London. (Annual).

Briggs G. *Civic & Corporate Heraldry - A Dictionary of Impersonal Arms.* Heraldry Today. Ramsbury 1971.

D'Allemagne H. *Les Accessoires du Costume, Vol. 1.* Paris 1935.

Debrett's Baronetage, Knightage & Companionage. Debrett's Peerage, London. (Annual).

Debrett's Peerage. Debrett's Peerage, London. (Annual).

Egan G. & Pritchard F. *Dress Accessories c1150-c1450.* HMSO London 1991.

Epstein D. *Buttons.* Studio Vista 1968.

Fairburn J. *Crests of the Families of Gt. Britain & Ireland.* New Orchard Editions. London 1986.

Fallon L. *Le Bouton Uniforme Française.* France 1915.

Froggatt D. J. *Railway Buttons, Badges & Uniforms.* Ian Allen Ltd. Shepperton 1986.

Hallows I.S. *Regiments & Corps of the British Army.* New Orchard Editions, London 1994.

Jackson, C. *Jackson's Gold & Silver Marks.* Antique Collectors' Club. Woodbridge. 1989.

Kaijser I., Nathorst-Böös E & Persson I-L. *Ur sjömannens kista och tunna, Wasastudier 10.* Tryckeri AB Grafisk Press Stockholm 1982.

Lightbown R.W. *Medieval European Jewellery.* Victoria & Albert Museum, London.

Luscomb S. *The Encyclopedia of Buttons.* Bonanza Books, New York 1967.

National Geographic January 1982.

Nöel Hume I. *Artifacts of Colonial America.* Vintage Books, New York 1991.

Parent A. *Le Bouton a Travers les Ages.* Paris 1935.

Parkyn H.G. *Shoulder-Belt Plates & Buttons.* Gale & Polden Ltd. Aldershot 1956.

Peacock P. *Buttons for the Collector.* David & Charles, Newton Abbott 1972.

Peacock P. *Discovering Old Buttons.* Shire Publications Ltd. Princes Risborough 1996

Pine L.G. *A Dictionary of Mottoes.* Routledge & Kegan Paul. London 1983.

Ripley H. *Buttons of the British Army 1855-1970.* Arms & Armour Press, London 1979.

Ripley H. *Police Buttons.* R. Hazell & Co. Henly-on-Thames 1983.

Ripley H. & Moodie R. *Local Militia Buttons.* Howard Ripley, Surbiton 1994.

Smith A.L. & Kent K. *The Complete Button Book.* World Work, Surrey 1949.

Squire G. *Buttons - A Guide for Collectors.* Frederick Muller Ltd. London 1972.

Squire G. *Livery Buttons - The Pitt Collection.* Leghorn Co., Pulborough 1976.

Thomas G. *Records of the Militia from 1757.* PRO Publications 1993.

Waugh N. *The Cut of Mens' Clothes 1600-1900.* Faber & Faber, London 1964.